Max
And his Big Imagination

⭐ SPACE ACTIVITY BOOK ⭐

by
Chrissy Metge

© Chrissy Metge 2019

www.chrissymetge.com
www.ducklingpublishing.com

All About Me

All about:

This is me:

I am ___ years old.

My favorite colour:

My birthday:

Max and his Big Imagination: Space Activity Book

WARM UP WORK

Follow the lines.

DRAW IN THE SHAPES

Fill in the shapes with anything you want!

5

Max and his Big Imagination: Space Activity Book

DRAW IN THE SHAPES

Fill in the shapes with anything you want!

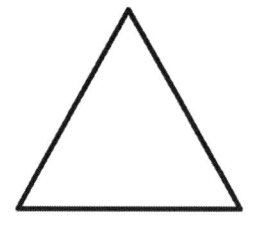

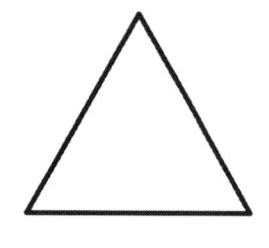

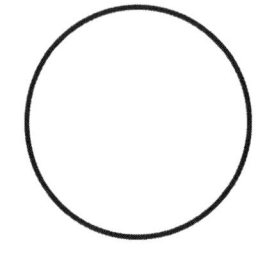

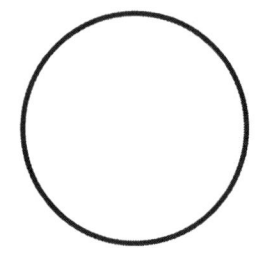

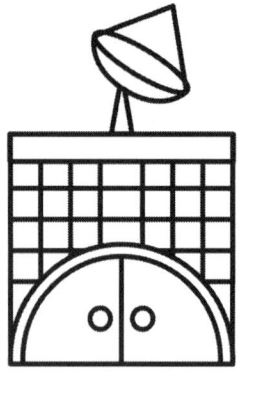

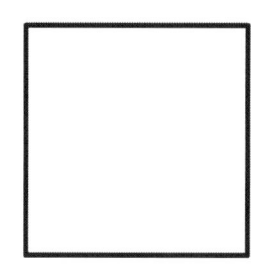

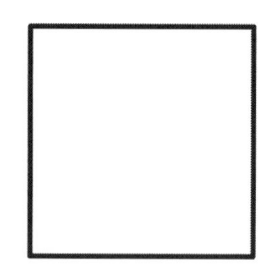

Max and his Big Imagination: Space Activity Book

COLOUR THE PLANETS

Use the colour key to colour the planets.

1 = red
2 = purple
3 = orange
4 = yellow
5 = green
6 = blue

HOW TO DRAW

Learn how to draw an alien!

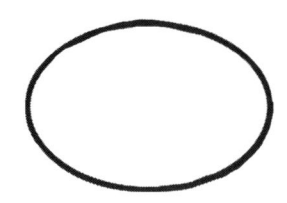

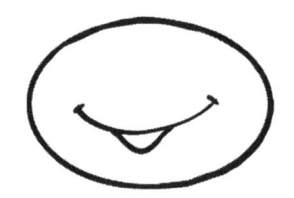

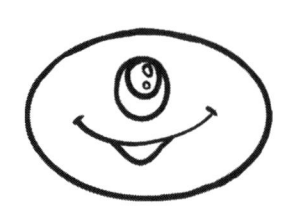

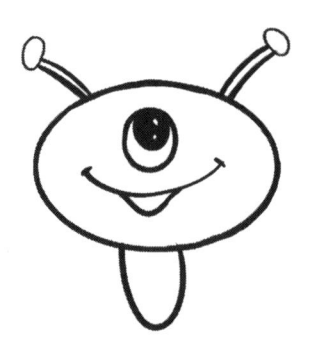

Max and his Big Imagination: Space Activity Book

HOW TO DRAW

Draw your alien here.

FINISH THE DRAWING

Design your own rocket ship.

10

Max and his Big Imagination: Space Activity Book

CONNECT THE DOTS

Connect the dots on the constellations.

The Swan

The Big Dipper

The Dog

The Dolphin

Max and his Big Imagination: Space Activity Book

FIND THE PATH

Find the path through the astronaut!

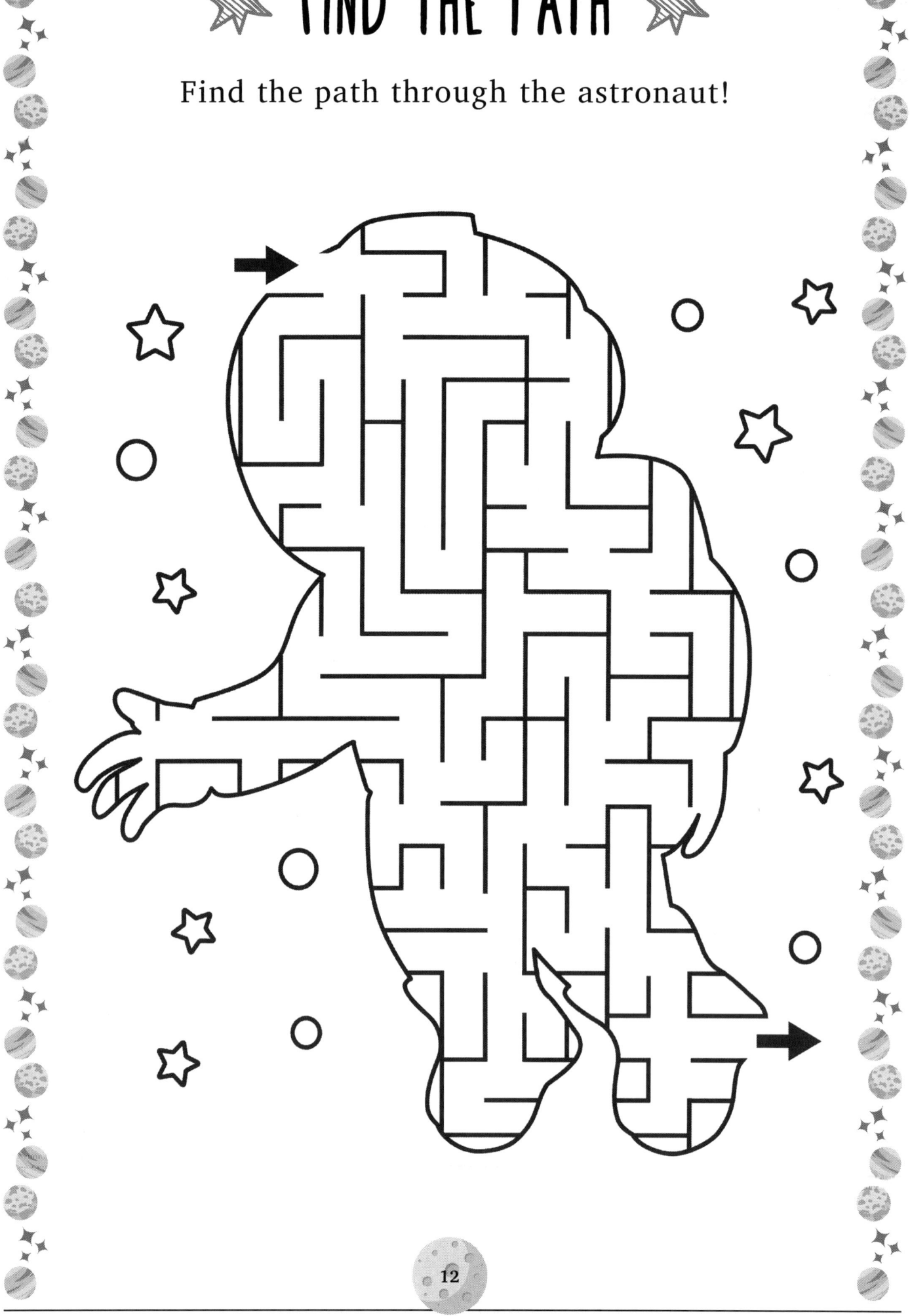

Max and his Big Imagination: Space Activity Book

TRACE THE LETTERS

Trace the letters on the rockets!

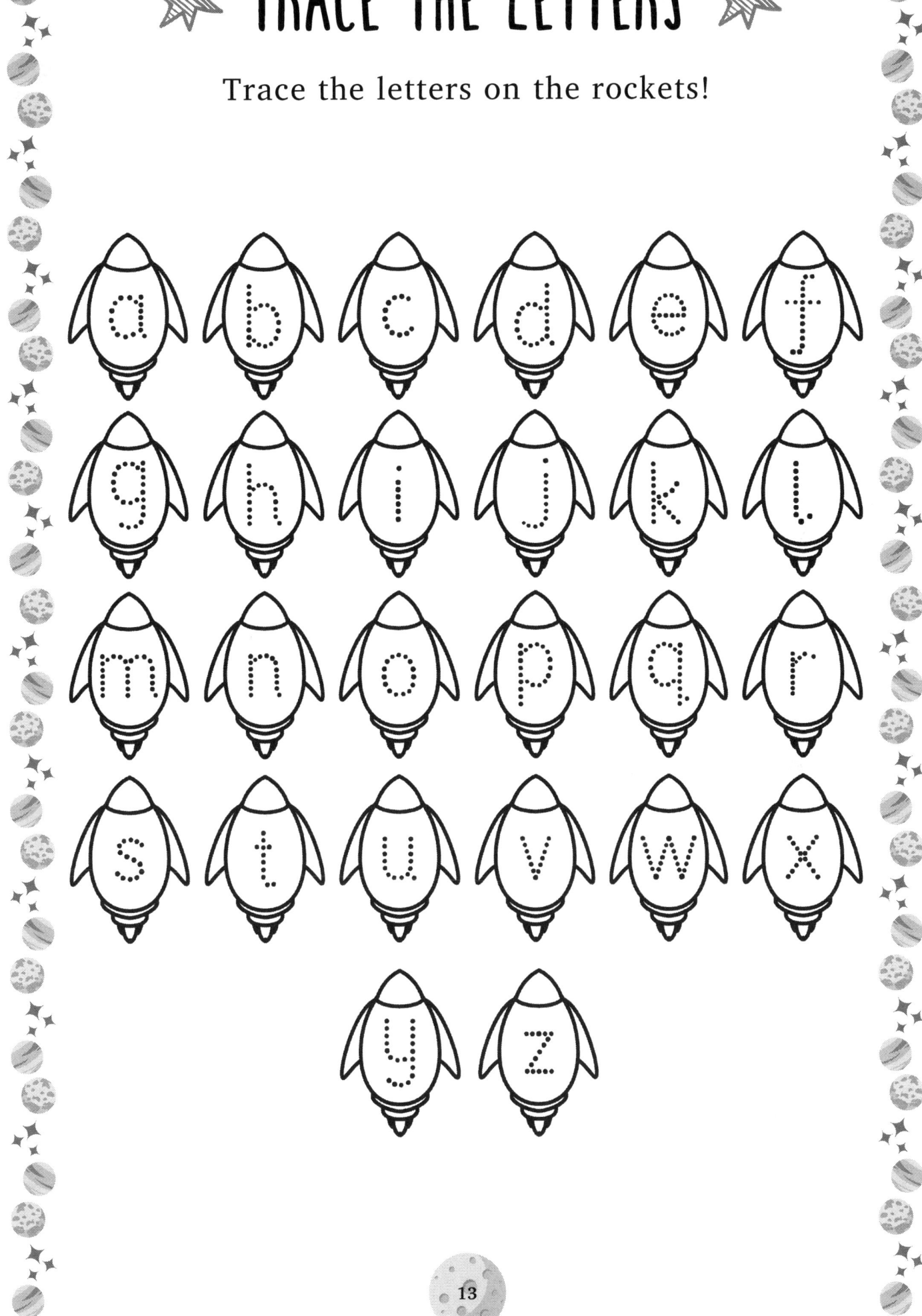

a b c d e f
g h i j k l
m n o p q r
s t u v w x
y z

HOW TO DRAW

Learn how to draw a rocket ship!

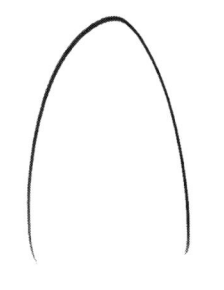

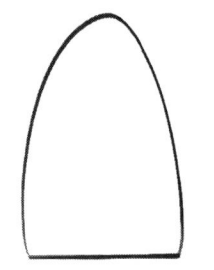

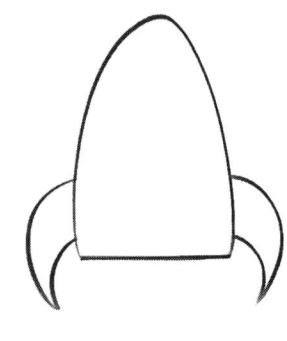

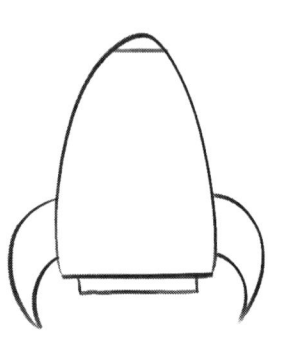

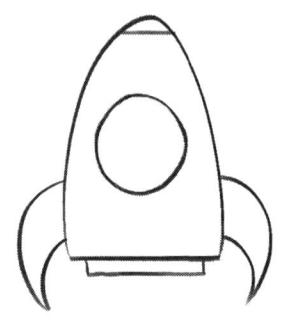

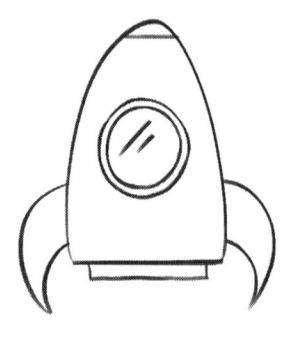

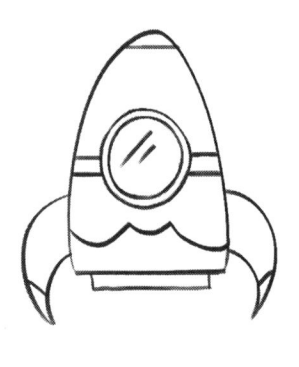

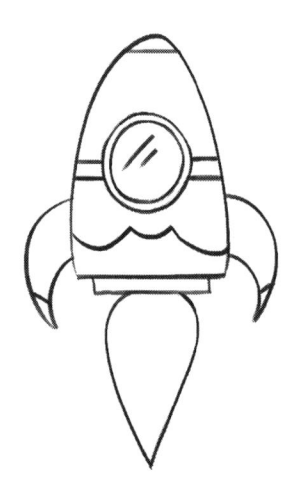

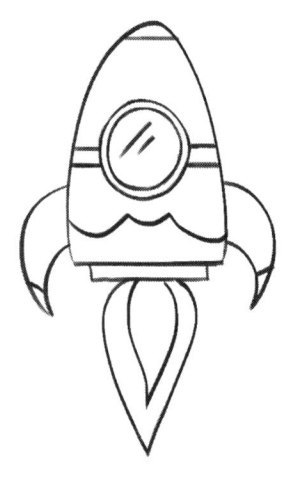

HOW TO DRAW

Draw your rocket ship here.

COLOUR THE PICTURE

Colour the planets and the stars!

Max and his Big Imagination: Space Activity Book

COLOUR THE STARS

Use the colour key to colour the stars.

1 = yellow   3 = brown   5 = orange   7 = grey   9 = pink
2 = blue   4 = red   6 = green   8 = purple   10 = white

Max and his Big Imagination: Space Activity Book

DESIGN YOUR OWN PLANET

Finish the pictures!

MY PLANET IS CALLED

....

Add your design here...

How many moons does your planet have?
....

Draw here

18

Max and his Big Imagination: Space Activity Book

NUMBER TRACE

Trace and write the numbers 0 to 10.

10	10	_____
9	9	_____
8	8	_____
7	7	_____
6	6	_____
5	5	_____
4	4	_____
3	3	_____
2	2	_____
1	1	_____
0	0	_____

COLOUR THE SATELLITE

Use the colour key to colour the satellite.

1 = blue   3 = grey   5 = yellow
2 = purple   4 = red

COUNTING PRACTICE

Draw a line between each number to match the object.

0
1
2
3
4
5
6

✩ DRAW A PICTURE ✩

Draw and colour the phases of the moon.

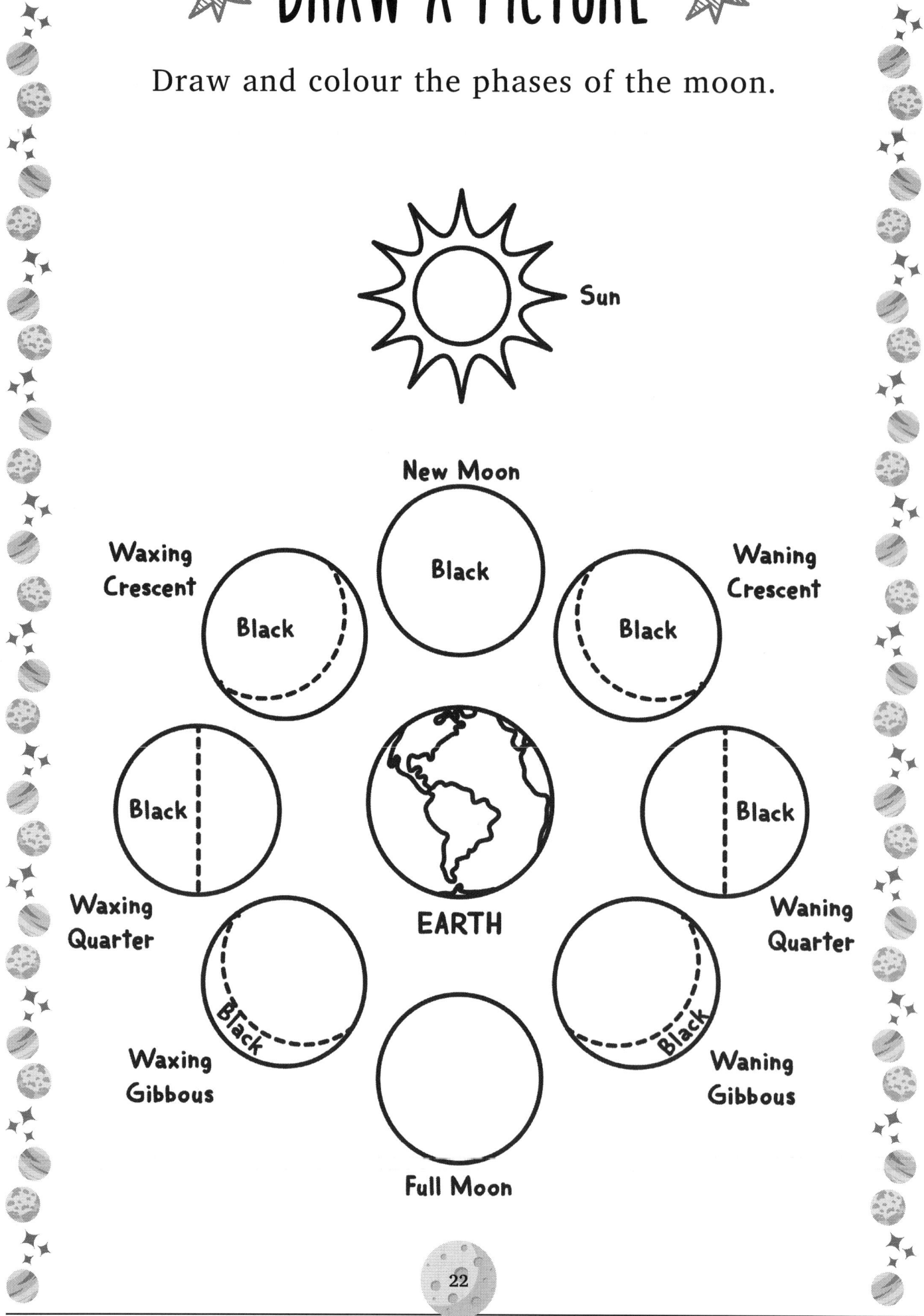

Sun

New Moon
Black

Waxing Crescent
Black

Waning Crescent
Black

Waxing Quarter
Black

EARTH

Waning Quarter
Black

Waxing Gibbous
Black

Waning Gibbous
Black

Full Moon

FINISH THE DRAWING

Draw a face inside the astronaut suit and colour the rest of the picture.

MY SPACE WORDS

Colour the space pictures.
Draw lines to match the words to the pictures.

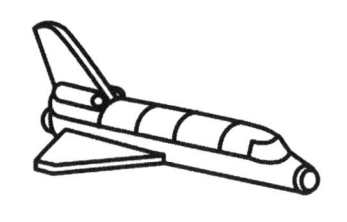

- Asteroid
- Shuttle
- Space Rover
- Planet
- Moon
- Sun
- Stars
- Astronaut

FINISH THE DRAWING

Draw a space station in the dome.

FIND THE PATH

Find the path through the rocket!

26

Max and his Big Imagination: Space Activity Book

DESIGN A CONSTELLATION

Connect any stars to design your own constellation.

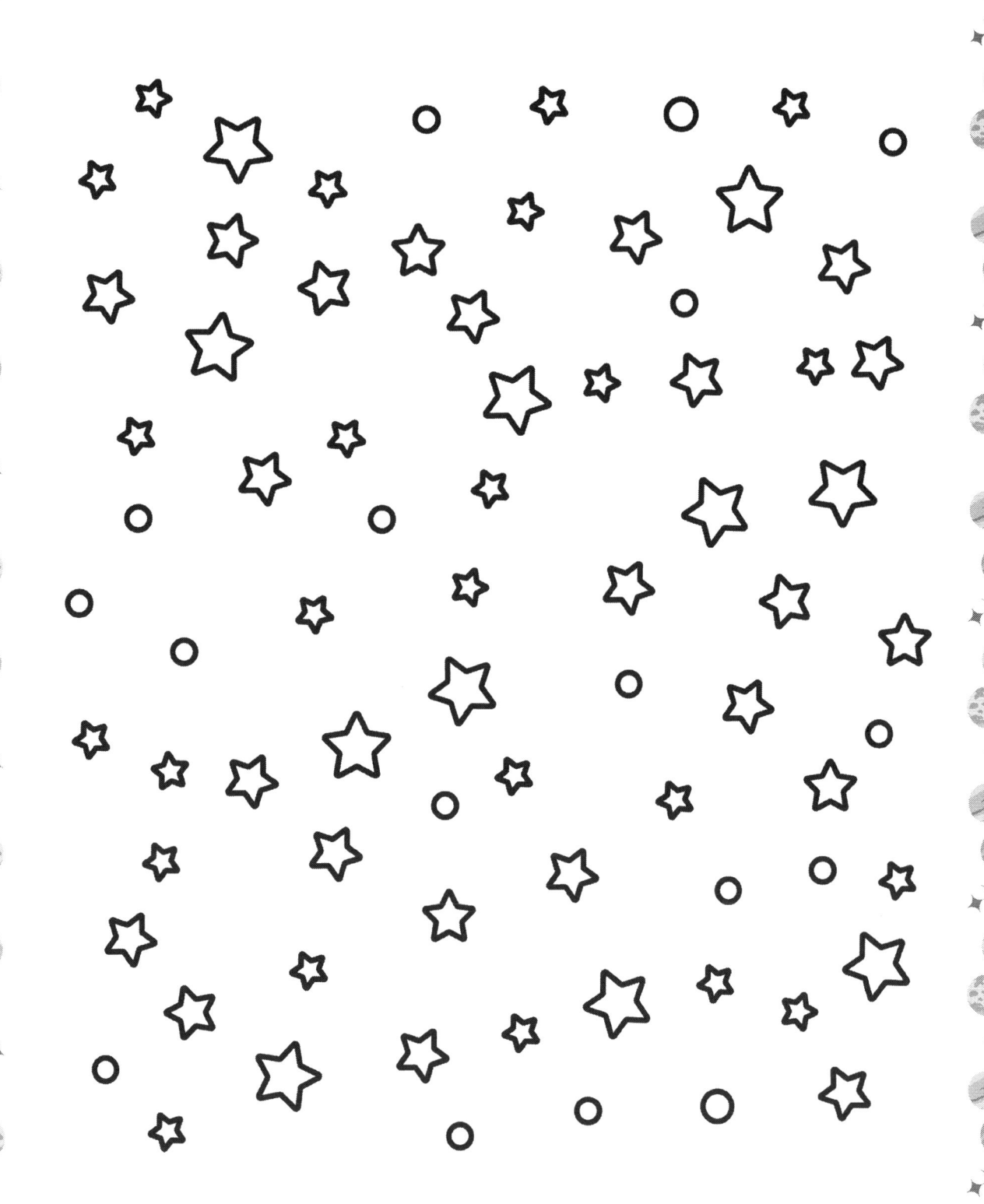

Name your constellation: ....

HOW TO DRAW

Learn how to draw a astronaut!

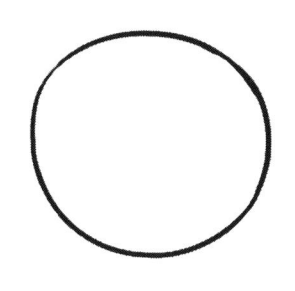

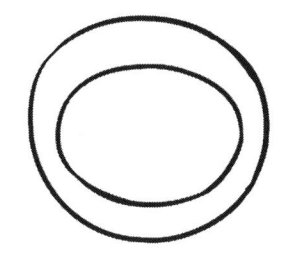

28

Max and his Big Imagination: Space Activity Book

HOW TO DRAW

Draw your astronaut here.

FIND THE PATH

Find the path through the maze!

30

Max and his Big Imagination: Space Activity Book

FIND, COUNT AND WRITE

Count and write the number of each item.

HOW TO DRAW

Learn how to draw a alien space ship!

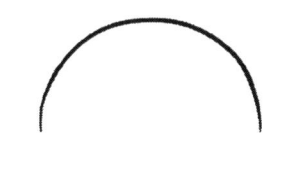

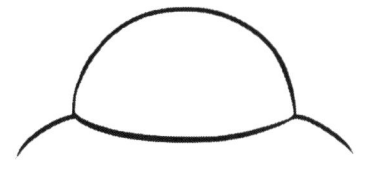

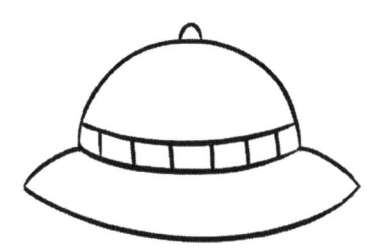

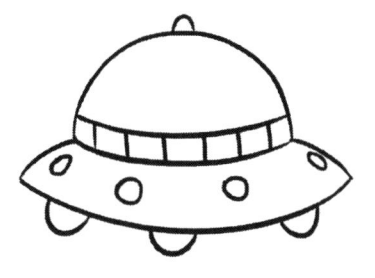

HOW TO DRAW

Draw your alien space ship here.

TRACE AND COLOUR

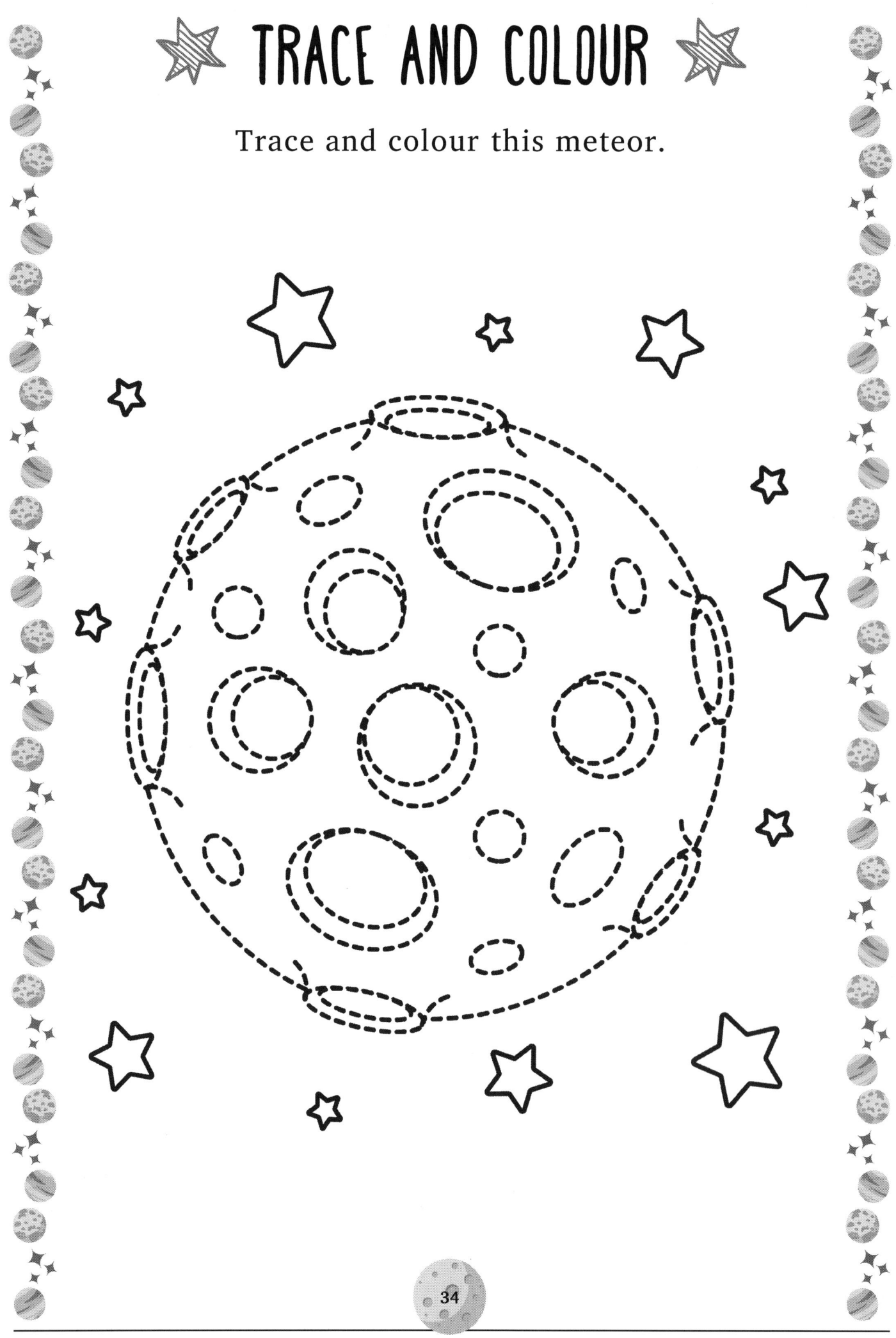

Trace and colour this meteor.

COLOUR AND CUT

Colour your own shooting star and cut it out.

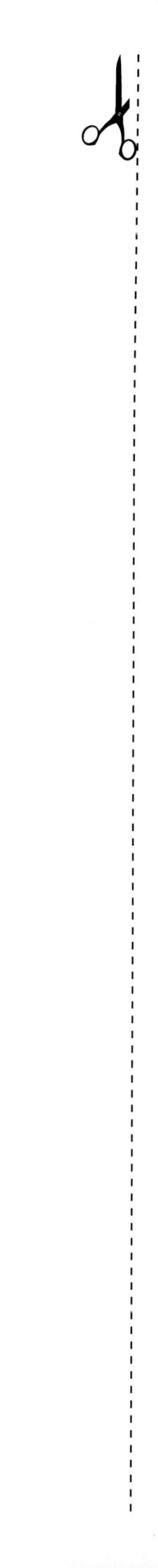

COLOUR AND CUT

Colour and cut out the planets, put them in their right place in space.

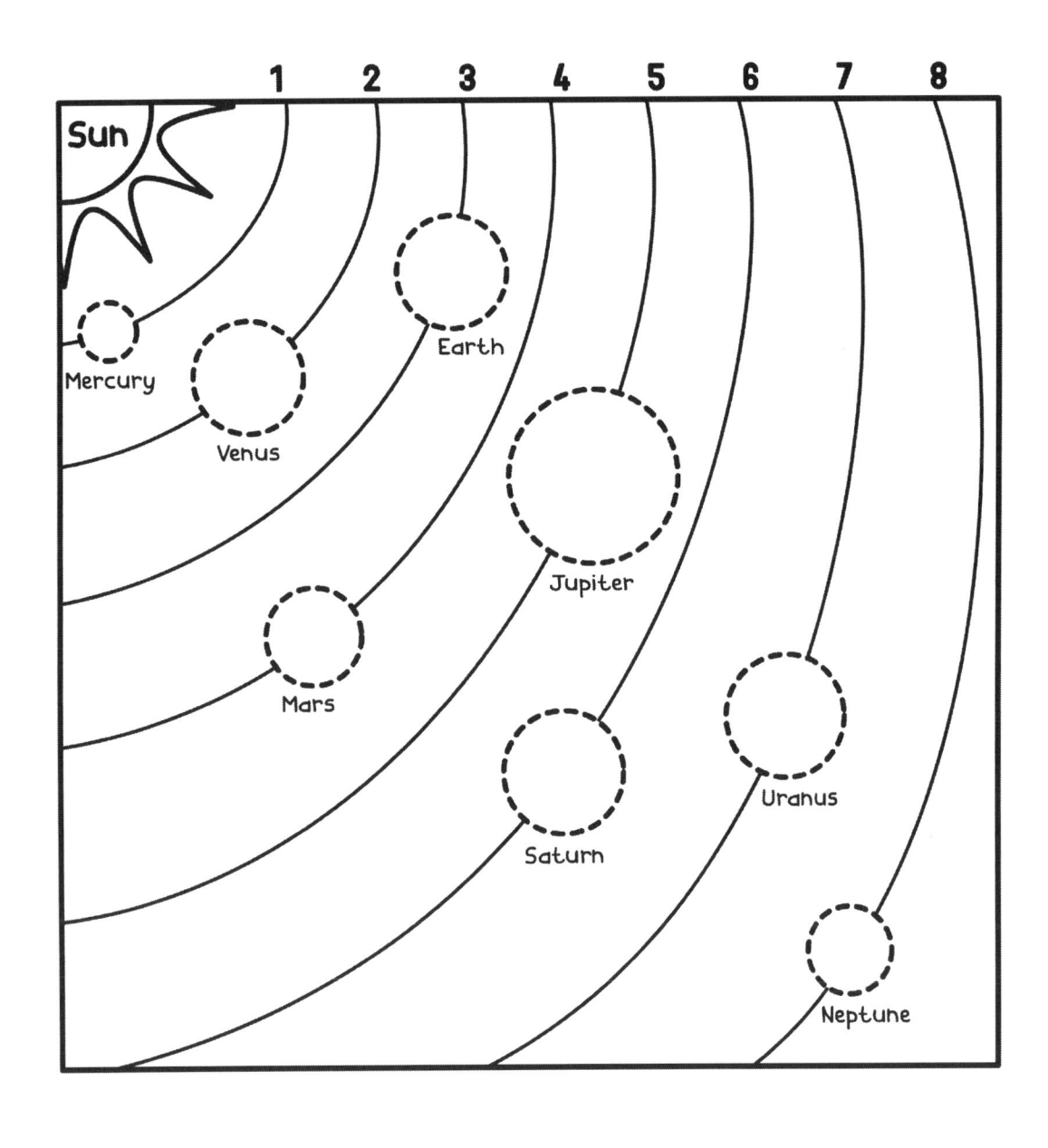

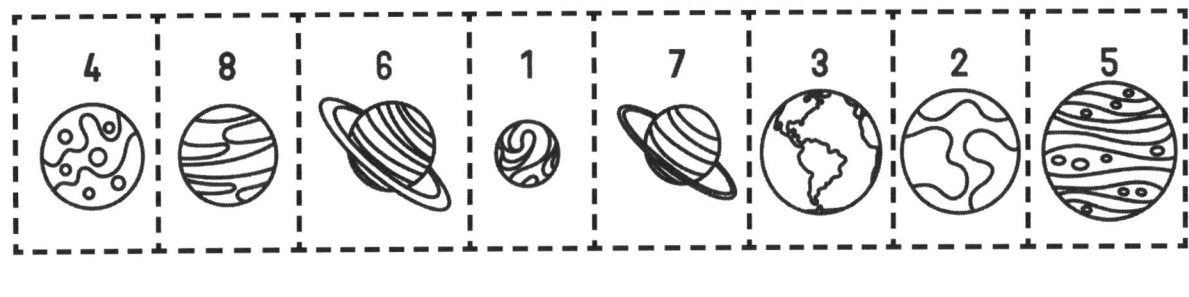

1 2 3 4 5 6 7 8

Sun

Mercury
Venus
Earth
Jupiter
Mars
Saturn
Uranus
Neptune

4 8 6 1 7 3 2 5

WHAT COMES NEXT?

Cut out and find the matching picture.

COLOUR A PICTURE

Colour and cut out the sun and planets to hang on your wall.

Sun

Mercury

Earth

Mars

Venus

Jupiter

Saturn

Neptune

Uranus

Max
And his Big Imagination

Check out our other activity books!

Transport Activity Book
Space Activity Book
Dinosaur Activity Book
Seaside Activity Book

Read, Play, Imagine!

www.ducklingpublishing.com